CAUGHT OFF GUARD
Twelve Tales of Surprise

by Bernard Jackson and Susie Quintanilla

The Peoples Publishing Group, Inc.

ISBN 0-88336-306-2

© 1990

The Peoples Publishing Group, Inc
299 Market Street
Saddle Brook, NJ 07663

All rights reserved. No part of this book may be reproduced or transmitted in any form or by any means, electronic or mechanical, including photocopying, recording, or by any information storage and retrieval system, without permission in writing from the publisher.

Printed in the United States of America

Edited by Maria A. Collis
Designed by Joanne M. Groth
Cover by Steve Rhodes
Illustrations by John D'Allaird

Table of Contents

1. **The Autopsy**
   - Word Study 4
   - Story 5

2. **The Grocery Store**
   - Word Study 10
   - Story 11

3. **The Problem Solver**
   - Word Study 16
   - Story 17

4. **The Price of Forgiveness**
   - Word Study 22
   - Story 23

5. **A Rainy Night**
   - Word Study 28
   - Story 29

6. **The Right Thing to Say**
   - Word Study 36
   - Story 37

7. **Pictures of Innocence**
   - Word Study 42
   - Story 43

8. **The Last Hope**
   - Word Study 48
   - Story 49

9. **The Lamp**
   - Word Study 54
   - Story 55

10. **The List**
    - Word Study 62
    - Story 63

11. **The Funny Man**
    - Word Study 68
    - Story 69

12. **The Receipt**
    - Word Study 74
    - Story 75

Word Study

autopsy (AW top see) medical examination of a dead body:
Sometimes, an *autopsy* is needed to discover the real cause of death.

examination (ex am in AY shun) a test or study of something:
The doctor gave him a physical *examination* to see if he was healthy.

grief (greef) sadness; *slang for* trouble:
Losing my wallet caused me a lot of *grief*.

identification (eye dent uh fuh KAY shun) *also* ID; proof of who someone is:
I carry *identification* when I want to cash a check.

incredible (in KREH duh bul) hard to believe:
Jack's story sounded *incredible*, but it was true.

medical examiner (MED uh kul eks AM uh ner) coroner; a public officer who examines dead bodies to learn the cause of death:
The *medical examiner* said that the woman had drowned.

organ (OR gun) one of several body parts that has a special function:
The heart is an *organ*.

publicity (puh BLIS uh tee) public attention:
The movie star enjoyed the *publicity* that he received everywhere he went.

victim (VIK tum) a person who is injured or killed:
The accident *victim* was rushed to the hospital.

1. The Autopsy

Dr. Peter Cross hated paperwork. It was the part of his job he liked the least. He hadn't thought he was going to like being a medical examiner at all. That was 15 years ago. Since then, he had changed his mind. Even now, he learned something new every day. But today, the paperwork was piled high on his desk. He signed another report and put it on top of a stack of finished reports.

"Dr. Cross, will you step in here a moment? I have something for you to look at," Dr. Helen Brown yelled from the examination room.

Helen Brown was new. She had just started working as a medical examiner last week. She was always asking questions.

"What do you want, Helen?" Dr. Cross yelled back.

"Please come here! It's the most amazing thing I've ever seen."

"What are you talking about, Helen?" Dr. Cross asked, as he walked into the room with his hands in his lab coat.

"The police brought this body in this morning. He was a hit-and-run victim. Look!" Dr. Brown pulled back the sheet. She had already started the autopsy. "Take a close look at the chest area. Isn't there something missing?"

"The heart's missing," Dr. Cross said. "Is this a joke, Helen? If it is, it isn't funny. You could get into a lot of hot water fooling around like this."

"Look again, Peter," she said nervously. "See what else is missing."

"I don't understand this," said Dr. Cross. "Where's the liver? And what are those organs, there? I've never seen organs like those before."

"I know. It's incredible." Dr. Brown's voice began to crack. "There's only one explanation I can think of."

The two doctors looked at each other.

"He's not a human being," said Dr. Cross.

"Exactly," said Dr. Brown. "And if he's not human, then what is he? And what am I supposed to write in my report?"

"Did he have any identification papers on him?" asked Dr. Cross.

"Yes, he had a wallet." Helen dropped the sheet back over the body. She walked over to a small table in the corner of the room. She brought back the wallet and opened it. The contents fell on the floor. She bent down and picked up the credit cards and the seven one-dollar bills.

"It says his name is Joseph Williams. It looks like he worked for a computer company. Here's his ID badge."

Dr. Cross looked at the badge in Helen's hand, but he wouldn't touch it.

"You know," he said. "It might be a good idea to forget what we've seen here. Sometimes things happen in the world that we can't explain. If you make this public—" He took a deep breath. "If you tell people you performed an autopsy on something that isn't human—" He stopped again to choose his words. "Things could go badly for you."

"What do you mean?" Helen asked.

"People might say that you messed up the autopsy. Even worse, they might say that you made the whole thing up. They'll say you're either a liar, or you're crazy."

"I can't just forget about it," Helen said. "I can't lie on an autopsy report. I never even cheated on a test in medical school. I don't know how. I just can't do it." She looked at Dr. Cross, then at the wallet in her hand. "Anyway, where there's one, there's bound to be more of them. They're out there for a reason." Helen rubbed her hand across the wallet. "I've got to find out what it is."

Dr. Cross could see from the look on her face that Helen Brown had made up her mind. He knew it was useless to argue with her.

"Do what you have to," he said. "But don't expect me to back you up." He turned and walked out.

Dr. Brown called the operator to get the telephone number of the computer company on Joseph Williams's badge. The operator said there was no listing for that company. She had three listings for "Joseph Williams." Dr. Brown called them all, but none turned out to be the right one.

Dr. Brown decided it was time to call the police.

7

A lieutenant named Peterson came to see her. Helen showed the lieutenant the body of Joseph Williams. Then she led Lieutenant Peterson into her office and showed him her autopsy report.

Lieutenant Peterson tapped his pencil on the top of Dr. Brown's desk. "Dr. Brown, what kind of a fool do you take me for? What you're suggesting is impossible. The only reason I can think of for all this is publicity. You want all the cameras and newspapers down here. You want to be famous, right?"

Dr. Brown shook her head "no" and stared at the autopsy report that lay on the desk between them.

"You want to be one of those hotshot doctors on TV, don't you? You think you can make a fortune. Write a book about it. They might even make a movie." Lieutenant Peterson laughed and put his feet up on Dr. Brown's desk. "Well, I'm not going to help you, Doc." He lit a cigar. He took a couple of long, lazy puffs, and tapped his ashes onto the floor.

"Please leave my office, Lieutenant," said Dr. Brown calmly. "I don't think we're going to get anywhere. I'm going to speak to your superior."

Lieutenant Peterson's face turned red with anger. He took his feet off Dr. Brown's desk and pounded it with his fist.

"Look, lady," he said. "You'll just buy yourself a world of grief. Don't think you can go over my head. The only cop over me is the chief. And he won't talk to you. Anyway, when I tell him the crazy story you told me— Well, we'll have a good laugh."

The lieutenant chuckled, coughed twice, and got up from the chair.

"You're a smart lady, Doc. Don't throw your career away." The lieutenant dropped his cigar on the floor and crushed it with his heel. "I'll check on you later, Doc." He unwrapped another cigar and dropped the wrapper on the floor as he left.

The next day, Dr. Helen Brown looked again at the autopsy report she had written.

"There's no way I can fight this thing alone," she said to herself. "The police aren't going to help. And I've tried every lead I had."

She decided she would have to lie. She took out another set of forms and began typing a new report.

"Helen, I think I've found something," Dr. Cross said. Dr. Brown looked up. Dr. Cross was standing in the doorway of her office. He was holding a wristwatch. Dr. Brown held out her hand. Dr. Cross walked up to her and handed her the watch.

"This watch was with the dead man's things," Dr. Cross said. "Look on the back. There's a number. It looks like a telephone number." He shrugged his shoulders. "Maybe it'll lead you to the others."

Helen smiled at him. He smiled back. Dr. Cross knew better than to take a chance with his own career. But he had felt bad about letting her down.

Helen was still smiling as she dialed the number. "This could be the lead I've been looking for!" she said.

At the other end of the line, the telephone rang three times before someone answered it.

"Police department. Lieutenant Peterson speaking."

Dr. Brown froze. Peterson's voice went on. "Hello? Who is this?... Hello!"

Dr. Brown slowly put the receiver down and turned back to her typewriter.

"Well, what was it?" Dr. Cross asked.

"Nothing," Dr. Brown said. "Wrong number."

Word Study

aisle (I'll) a passage in a store, restaurant, or theater for people to walk through:
Tuna can be found in the canned foods *aisle* of the supermarket.

checker (CHEK er) an employee in a store who totals the cost of purchases and collects payment for them:
The *checker* turned the box of frozen vegetables over and over, but she couldn't find a price tag.

customer (KUS tuh mer) a person who buys something:
"Do you have this shirt in red?" the *customer* asked.

loudspeaker (LOWD SPEEK er) a device that projects sound through a room or area:
The principal's voice came over the *loudspeaker*, calling all the students to the assembly.

page (paj) to try to find someone by calling his or her name:
"I'll be away from my desk for a while," the man told his secretary. "Please *page* me if my wife calls."

2. The Grocery Store

Tom pushed the cart with a bad wheel up one aisle and down the next. The aisles were crowded. He had to be careful not to run over some children who were hanging on their mother's cart. He stopped for a moment to recheck the grocery list. He wanted to be sure he hadn't forgotten anything.

"Let's see, milk, a loaf of bread and two cans of vegetable soup. Hmmm," he said to himself. "Something is missing."

Tom suddenly remembered that his wife had told him to get pork and beans. They were on sale. He made his way past the other shoppers in the canned foods aisle. Tom finally found the pork and beans and threw several cans into his cart. It was time to leave.

"Alex, please come to the front and check," said a voice over the loudspeaker.

Tom rolled his cart to the front of the store. There were 16 check-out lanes, but they were all empty. There wasn't a checker in sight. In fact, there wasn't even a customer in sight. Tom looked around. The store had been full of people when he came in. Now there was no sign of life except for a light over one of the check-out lanes to show that it was open. Tom rolled his cart to that check-out lane and waited for the checker to come.

"Alex, please come to the front," said the voice over the loudspeaker.

Tom waited another five minutes. It was getting dark outside. The loudspeaker paged Alex three more times.

Tom was just about to give up and go home when a dark-haired boy about 16 years old came running down the aisle. When he reached Tom, the boy went behind the check-out counter. The badge on the boy's shirt said "Alex."

"Hey, I'm really sorry," the boy said to Tom.

"I didn't think you were coming," Tom said.

"I just heard them page me," Alex said. "I was busy stacking boxes in the back room. I get off work in two hours, and I have to get all those boxes put away before I leave."

"No problem," Tom said, smiling. He was glad to finally be getting out of the store. He helped Alex bag the groceries.

The display on the cash register said $6.42. Tom quickly wrote a check and handed it to the boy.

"See you later," Alex said with a smile, as Tom hurried out the door.

On the way home, Tom had a strange feeling. Somehow things around him seemed different. The sign in front of the gas station had changed. Gas was 10 cents higher. It also seemed a lot lighter outside than it had when he was waiting in the store.

Finally, Tom pulled into his driveway and turned off the engine. He leaned over and grabbed the bag of groceries on the seat next to him. He got out of the car and walked to the front door. He shifted the bag of groceries to one arm. Before Tom could put his key in the lock, Carol, his wife, opened the door. Tom walked in. Carol looked at him, and her mouth fell open. Then her eyes filled with tears.

"Tom? Tom! Where have you been?" She hugged Tom's neck fiercely and sobbed. Tom dropped the bag of groceries, and the contents tumbled on to the floor.

"Tom, where on earth have you been? I thought you were dead," she said, weeping softly in his ear.

"Honey, I just went to the store. There was only one checker, and I had to wait for him for a long time. But I'm not *that* late. Why are you so upset? I've only been gone a couple of hours."

Carol stepped back and looked at him. There were still tears in her eyes. She put her hands on her hips.

"You left here two years ago to get milk, a loaf of bread, two cans of vegetable soup, and some pork and beans. You didn't come back. I reported you missing the next day. Everyone thinks you're dead. I thought you were dead, too. The police asked me if you would just go away. I told them you could never do anything like that." She paused a long moment. "Where have you been?"

Tom looked down at the pile of groceries at his feet. Then he looked at his wife. "I just went to the store. I couldn't have been gone more than two hours. I swear I don't know what you're talking about!"

He stepped over the groceries and went into the living room. He sat on the couch. Carol followed him and just stood, staring at her husband.

"Two years!" Tom said. "How can this be? I don't understand. What year is this?"

"It's 1989," Carol said, sitting down next to him.

"It can't be 1989, Carol." Tom shook his head. "It's 1987. It's 1987!"

They both looked at each other for a long time. Finally, Tom spoke. "Let's go. I want to see something." He grabbed Carol's hand and pulled her off the couch.

"Where are we going?" asked Carol.

"We're going to find out where I've been for the last two years."

They silently drove in the direction of the grocery store. Tom pulled up in front of the store. The large windows were boarded up. The sidewalk glistened with pieces of broken glass. A small sign on the door read "For Sale Or Lease. Call Clark Realty." Tom and Carol got out of the car and walked toward the locked doors.

"I was just here, Carol." Tom jerked the door handle. "I was just here a few minutes ago. This can't be!"

"Tom, this place has been closed for almost two years. You disappeared, and there was someone else, too. People started to say the store was haunted. They closed the store because people stopped coming."

"You said there was someone else?"

"Alex Ramos disappeared the same day you did. He was working in the back of the store. The store got busy, and they called him to check groceries. He never came. They looked all over for him, just like they looked for you." Carol sighed. "Poor Alex. I don't think his parents will ever get over it."

Tom shook his head. "It still doesn't make any sense," he said. "But I'll bet you one thing."

"What's that?"

"I bet Alex will come back."

"Why do you say that?" Carol asked.

Tom smiled. "It took me two years to get home, and I was just out grocery shopping," he said. "Alex doesn't get off work for another hour and a half."

Word Study

autopsy (AW top see) medical examination of a dead body:
The *autopsy* showed that the woman had drowned.

chemical (KEM uh kul) a substance made by or used in a chemical process:
Some packaged foods have a *chemical* in them to keep them fresh.

intolerable (in TOL er uh bul) too hard or painful to be endured:
When he broke his leg, the pain was *intolerable*.

jealous (JEL us) suspicious; distrustful:
Mr. Cook is *jealous* of his wife's family and friends.

liquid (LIK wid) a substance that flows and may be poured from its container:
Water is *liquid* at room temperature, but becomes solid when it freezes.

similar (SIM uh ler) alike, but not completely the same:
The two women's dresses were *similar*, only one had a higher collar.

solution (suh LOO shun) an answer to a problem:
He worked for an hour to find the *solution* to the math problem.

withdrawal (with DRAW ul) the act of taking away or removing:
Did you make a *withdrawal* from the bank to buy groceries today?

3. The Problem Solver

Harry knocked on the door of the apartment. He could hear footsteps behind the door. The doorknob turned. The door opened, and a young woman stood in front of him. She smiled vaguely.

"Yes?"

"Mr. Jones sent me." Harry extended his hand, but the young woman ignored it.

"Please come in," she said. She looked down the hallway and closed the door behind Harry.

"Please have a seat, sir," she said.

Harry sat down on a metal chair. It felt cold under him. There was no furniture in the apartment except a table and some folding chairs. Harry noticed a large picture window that faced the parking lot. The young woman sat down at the table across from him.

"My name is Mrs. Raffle. Mr. Jones told me you were coming."

"Yes, Mr. Jones told me—I mean—" Harry cleared his throat and began again. "Mr. Jones told me that you have certain chemicals. He said you could help me with a problem I have."

"What kind of problem are you having?"

"It's my wife."

"What's the problem with your wife?" Mrs. Raffle leaned over and dug a nail file out of her purse. "The chemicals I have are for very special purposes. They're also very expensive."

"My wife is a very jealous person, Mrs. Raffle. It makes life intolerable. I used to like it. The jealousy, I mean. But she's gone crazy with it. If I come home late from work, she wants to know what kept me. One day my car broke down, and I couldn't get to a phone. She called the police and reported me missing! Can you believe that? I can't go fishing with my friends because she starts crying and says I don't love her. I don't know what to do. My friend, Mr. Jones, suggested I talk to you. He had a similar problem, and you helped him."

"I just may have the solution to your problem." Mrs. Raffle reached into her purse again and brought out a small bottle. "This is what I gave your friend."

"What is it?"

"Come, now. You know what it is. It's a colorless, tasteless liquid. You can put it in any drink. A few drops of this in coffee, tea, or any other drink will do the trick."

"A poison, Mrs. Raffle?"

"A problem solver, sir. A problem solver. People have problems. I offer solutions. It's very simple."

"Won't an autopsy show that she was poisoned?"

Mrs. Raffle leaned back in her chair.

"There's the magic, sir," she said. "You can buy poison anywhere. But to find a poison that leaves no trace is almost impossible. For this reason, it is very expensive."

"It sounds like just the thing I need. How much is it?"

"Five thousand dollars. Not a penny less."

"Mr. Jones told me it would cost five thousand dollars." Harry started counting out money from an envelope. "I was hoping I had heard him wrong."

Mrs. Raffle didn't say anything. She watched carefully as Harry counted out the five thousand dollars.

* * *

Harry threw his briefcase on the hall table and loosened his tie.

"Margaret, I'm home," he yelled into the kitchen.

"I'm fixing dinner, Harry," said a voice from the kitchen.

A moment later, Margaret walked out of the kitchen carrying a glass of iced tea.

"Where have you been? Why are you so late? What happened?" she said.

"I had to make a little stop to see one of our customers," Harry said. "Besides, Margaret, I'm not that late."

"OK, dear. No problem," Margaret said, handing him the iced tea.

Harry was surprised. He had expected Margaret to fight with him for being late.

"What did you do today?" he asked, taking a sip of iced tea.

"Nothing very interesting. I just went to the bank," she said. "I fixed a little snack for you."

She pointed to a tray of cheese and crackers on the coffee table. "I know how hungry you always get just before dinner."

"Oh, I'm not really hungry." Harry sat down on the couch and put his feet on the coffee table. He knew that Margaret hated it when he put his feet on the table. "In a couple of hours," he thought, "she won't be getting mad at anyone—ever again." He smiled and popped a cracker into his mouth. The salty cracker made him thirsty, and he took a big swallow of iced tea. Then he noticed something on the floor next to the coffee table. He reached down and picked it up.

"Margaret, what's this piece of paper? It was on the floor."

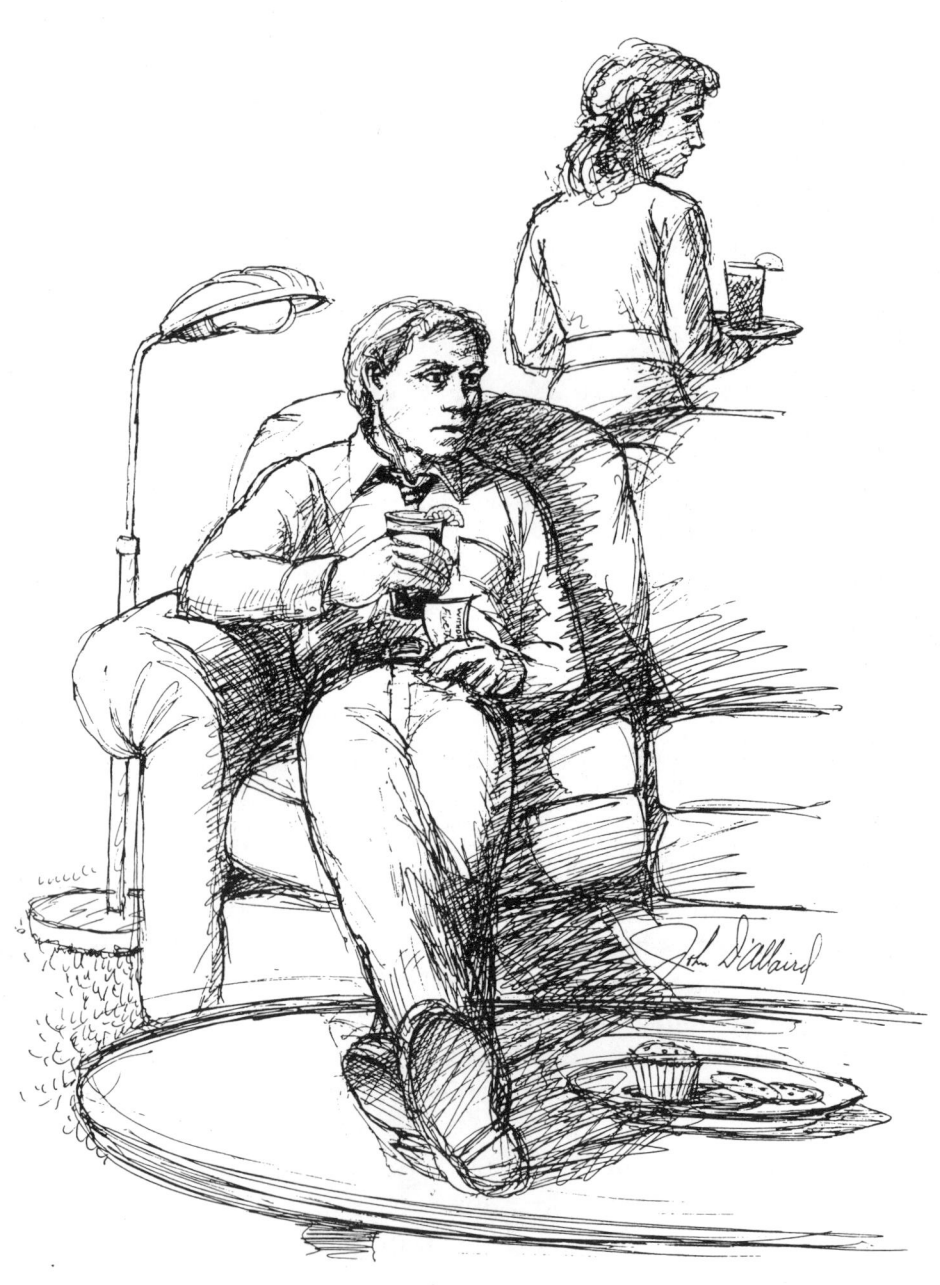

"Oh, that," Margaret said, reaching for the paper. Harry pulled it back and studied it. Margaret dropped her hand to her side.

"Why, I guess it's a bank withdrawal slip," she said. "I must have dropped it."

She shrugged her shoulders and went back into the kitchen.

"Margaret," Harry called after her. "This slip says you took five thousand dollars out of our savings account. What in the world did you buy for five thousand dollars?"

Margaret's voice came sweetly from the kitchen.

"Finish your tea, Harry. I'll tell you after dinner."

Word Study

confession (kon FESH shun) the telling of one's sins:
The police detective taped the man's *confession* to the burglary.

conscience (KON shunss) a feeling that one must do right or be good:
Her *conscience* bothered her when she told a lie.

delusion (dee LOO zhun) something unreal or false that is believed, especially by a person who is mentally ill:
John speaks French all the time because he suffers from the *delusion* that he is the king of France.

hit-and-run having to do with a road accident in which the guilty driver does not stop to help:
Nobody saw the *hit-and-run* accident that killed two people.

medication (med uh KAY shun) medicine:
The woman took *medication* for her headaches.

penance (PEN unss) something done to show sadness or regret for one's sins:
The boy stayed after school as a *penance* for cheating on his spelling test.

superintendent (soo per in TEN dunt) person in charge:
The *superintendent* of the building made sure the garbage was put out.

ward (woard) a section or large room in a hospital where patients who need similar treatment stay:
The children's *ward* is on the third floor of the hospital.

4. The Price of Forgiveness

Dr. Anderson walked down the hall of St. Luke's General Hospital. He noticed that the walls looked dull. He made a mental note to call the building superintendent. She had promised him that they were going to start painting that hall this week. It was already Wednesday. He pushed open the swinging door and entered the ward.

The mental ward at St. Luke's was not like any of the other mental wards that Dr. Anderson had seen. Here, every effort was made to make the atmosphere cheery and bright. The lighting was soft, not harsh as in other parts of the hospital. The furniture was painted bright colors.

Dr. Anderson knocked on the door of his third patient of the day.

"Come in, Father," said a voice from behind the door.

Dr. Anderson pushed on the door lightly and stepped into the room. "How are you feeling today, Mr. Brock?"

"Father, I asked you to come, and you came. How kind of you."

"How are you feeling?" repeated Dr. Anderson.

"I'm fine, Father. I'm just old and tired," said Mr. Brock.

"Oh, you're not so old," said Dr. Anderson. He patted Mr. Brock's hand and looked at his chart. "Some people live to be a hundred."

"I'm getting close to the end," said Mr. Brock. "I know it. Some things you just know, Father. Like the way you know that God sees everything."

Dr. Anderson shifted his weight nervously, from one foot to the other. Mr. Brock had been admitted last week. He was having delusions. His latest delusion was that Dr. Anderson was his family priest.

"How's the family?" Dr. Anderson asked, trying to change the subject.

"I guess they're all right. My daughter called the other day. She said that she would come to see me. She hasn't. She and her husband were supposed to leave for Europe today. Maybe they'll come and see me after they get back. I never got out of the United States, Father. I was always afraid something might happen to me, and they would bury me in some foreign country. I don't think my soul could stand that."

"How about your son?"

"He's doing OK. Of course, it's been several years since I last saw him. He calls me once in a while. But I didn't send for you to tell you about my children. I want you to hear my confession, Father."

"Confession?" Dr. Anderson said. It was bad enough that Mr. Brock thought he was a priest. Listening to a confession was something he was not prepared to do, even as a doctor. "Oh, no. I couldn't—"

"Father, I have to get this off my chest. I've carried it inside me for twenty years. Now I want to die, and I want to die in peace. I want a clear conscience."

"If it's some little thing—God will forgive—" Dr. Anderson fumbled for words.

"It's not a little thing, Father. Twenty years ago today, I killed someone."

"You killed someone?" Dr. Anderson moved closer.

"Yes."

Dr. Anderson knew he shouldn't let Mr. Brock talk on. Nothing good would come of it, he told himself. Still, he looked at the old man's face and asked, "Who?"

"That's the worst part," said Mr. Brock. "I don't even remember his name. It happened so long ago. My memory just isn't so good, anymore. I almost think it was a dream sometimes, that it didn't really happen."

"What didn't really happen?" Dr. Anderson's voice was calm.

"I was driving home late from work. It was dark, around nine-thirty. I was very sleepy. The road was wet. I remember that, because the headlights made the road look shiny and slick. I must have dozed off. And my head must have fallen forward onto the steering wheel, because the horn woke me. I looked up. My car was heading toward the shoulder of the road. There was another car ahead, a parked car. A man stood next to it, on the driver's side, holding a tire. He must have been getting ready to change the tire. I saw him for an instant in the light from my headlights. I didn't have time to stop. He looked surprised, not scared or anything, just surprised. I've never been able to forget that face, not for twenty years."

"You mean it was an accident?"

"I didn't mean to hit him, Father. I saw his name in the paper the next day, and I was sick. If only I hadn't worked so late—if only I'd been playing the radio—maybe the whole thing would never have happened."

"You say, you can't even remember his name?" said Dr. Anderson. The old man shook his head. Dr. Anderson looked at his watch. It was time to move on to the next patient, or he wouldn't finish his rounds in time. "Where did it happen?" he asked.

"On the Old Bay Highway. I didn't report it, Father."

"Did you say Old Bay Highway?"

"Yes, Father. Please forgive me." Mr. Brock's eyes filled with tears.

Dr. Anderson moved to the window. He looked out at the parking lot. He saw his car there. "You said it was twenty years ago? Twenty years ago, today?"

"Yes, Father. I didn't stop. I didn't mean to hit him, Father."

Dr. Anderson turned and walked toward the old man.

"Why didn't you stop to help him?" the doctor said. "To see if he was still alive?" His voice was calm, but his hands were shaking. He grabbed Mr. Brock by the shoulders. "Why didn't you stop?"

"I was scared, Father."

Dr. Anderson began shaking the old man by his shoulders. "Why?" he said again. "Why?!?"

"I don't know. I've always tried to do the right thing, Father. Please forgive me, Father!"

Dr. Anderson stopped shaking him and looked at Mr. Brock's face. He looked at his own hands clenched tight around the old man's shoulders. He dropped his arms to his sides and looked away. His eyes filled with tears. He walked back to the window and picked up Mr. Brock's chart from the windowsill.

"Please forgive me," Mr. Brock begged softly.

"I don't do the forgiving, Mr. Brock," said Dr. Anderson.

"Are you going to give me a penance to do, Father?"

Dr. Anderson closed the blinds on the window. The morning sun was hitting Mr. Brock in the eyes. He wrote a note on his chart. "You've already done your penance, Mr. Brock. I'll see you tomorrow."

Dr. Anderson walked back to the nurses' station. He handed the nurse his clipboard. "I want to change Mr. Brock's medication. He's starting to come out of some of his delusions."

"Does he still think you're a priest?" said the nurse, laughing.

"Yes. And it's not at all funny, Nurse." Dr. Anderson's voice cracked with emotion. "I don't want you laughing at these patients."

"I'm sorry, Doctor."

There was a long silence between them.

"What's the matter, Doctor?" the nurse asked. "You don't seem like yourself today."

Dr. Anderson leaned on the counter of the nurses' station. He looked at his hands.

"I'm sorry. I get like this every year," he said. "It was twenty years ago today that a hit-and-run driver killed my father on the Old Bay Highway."

Word Study

convenience store (kun VEEN yunss stor) a small grocery store, usually open late at night and early in the morning:
Does the gas station on the corner have a *convenience store* attached to it?

counter (KOWN ter) in a store or restaurant, a level surface on which goods are sold or meals are served:
If we eat at the *counter*, we'll get faster service.

downpour (DOWN por) a heavy rain:
The afternoon *downpour* flooded the streets.

resolved (re ZALVD) decided:
I *resolved* never to go on another blind date.

supervisor (SOO per vie zur) a person who oversees and directs others:
If you do a good job at work, you might be made a *supervisor*.

tiresome (TIRE sum) boring; tedious:
We went straight to bed after the long, *tiresome* drive.

5. A Rainy Night

The young clerk wiped the counter for the 10th time. It was a tiresome chore, but he was getting used to it. His supervisor had come in the day before.

"Make sure the counter's clean," the supervisor had said. "It's very important to have a clean counter. People don't like a dirty counter. Our studies show it."

The supervisor was always talking about studies and what they showed. Jason wadded up the rag and threw it in the small basin next to the cash register. He looked up. The front of the convenience store was all glass. Through the glass he could see that it was starting to rain.

The weather forecast had said to expect a thunderstorm, so Jason wasn't surprised. It had said something about a cold front and a warm front coming together. He looked at his watch. It was one o'clock in the morning. Only one more hour, and he could close the store. Jason liked the new store hours. Closing at two o'clock was much better than at four. Very few people came into the Mighty Mart convenience store after midnight. When they did, it was just for cigarettes or a can of soda.

Closing at midnight would be even better, he thought. He resolved to mention it to his supervisor. "He'll probably just tell me what the studies show," Jason said aloud.

Jason sat down on a tall stool behind the counter. He made a mental list of the things he had left to do: Mop the floor. Check the dates on the milk in the cooler. Fill out the cash register report.

Just then, the headlights of a car pulled into the small parking lot. They were all Jason could see of the car.

Probably someone on their way home from the second shift at the plant, he thought.

The door of the car opened. An umbrella popped open, and a dark figure moved under it. Lightning struck somewhere. A few seconds later, Jason heard the thunder. The rain was coming down harder. The door of the convenience store flew open with great force as the shadowy figure entered, umbrella first.

"Wow, it's sure tough out there tonight," said the man. "I didn't think it was going to rain this hard."

He was a middle-aged man. His clothes looked old. He wiped his feet on the floor mat in front of the door. He closed his umbrella and shook the rain from it. The water gathered in a small pool at his feet.

"Sorry about the water," he said.

"No problem. I gotta mop after a while, anyway."

"I've been on the road a long time. I figured I'd stop and get some coffee. Got any?"

"Sure," Jason said. "It's not too fresh, though. I don't get many customers this time of night." Jason pointed to the coffee pot next to the cooler.

"Thanks."

The man stamped his feet one last time on the mat in front of the door. He leaned his umbrella next to the magazine rack. Another pool of water started to form.

"My name's Skinner," said the man as he poured the stale coffee into a plastic cup.

"Oh," said Jason, surprised. Customers usually didn't introduce themselves.

Skinner emptied three packets of sugar into the coffee and stirred it. Then he walked to the front of the store and looked out the window. Lightning struck again in the distance. The thunder rolled in a few seconds later. Skinner kept looking out at the parking lot. He didn't turn before he spoke.

"I'm your father, Jason," he said.

"What?" Jason jumped down from his stool. He thought he must have heard wrong.

Skinner turned and looked at the young man. He walked to the counter. He put one hand in his pocket and brought out a 50-cent piece. He flipped it in the air, and it landed on the counter next to the cash register. Jason put his hand on the coin, still staring at Skinner.

"Yes, I'm your father," Skinner said. "I know that's hard to believe, but it's true."

"What are you talking about?" Jason said.

Skinner paused and nodded. He looked away. Jason's eyes reminded him of Marie, the boy's mother.

"I know it's hard to believe," Skinner said again. He started to pace back and forth between the counter and the front windows.

"You see, I married your mother, but it didn't work out," Skinner said. "I tried. I really tried, but it just didn't work out." He took a sip of coffee. "Marie, your mother, was a fine woman. It's just that I was always on the road. It was the only life I knew.

"When your mom divorced me, I just stayed on the road. I didn't even know about you until years later. I always meant to come by and meet you. But you know how it is. When you're traveling all the time, one year just passes into another."

He stopped and looked at Jason. Then he looked away again, out to the parking lot.

"I wanted to come when I heard that your mother was dying. But I never made it." Skinner took another sip of coffee and cleared his throat. "Being on the road is a tough life, son. You can make a lot of money, but it *takes* a lot of money. And it takes a lot out of you.

"I looked your name up in the phone book," he said, starting to pace again. "I called your apartment, and your roommate told me where you were."

Jason leaned forward. His hand still covered the coin his father had tossed onto the counter.

"Why did you come here?" Jason asked. "After all these years, what do you want?"

"Nothing. I don't want anything from you." Skinner folded his arms and hung his head. "I just thought you'd like to know who your father was," he whispered.

Skinner took a last sip of coffee and threw the cup in the trash.

"I guess I shouldn't have come here," he said. "It's just that I'm on my way to California. I might not get another chance. I just wanted to see you." He took a last look at Jason, then picked up his umbrella and opened the door. The wind howled and blew open the covers of the magazines on the rack by the door.

"Wait!" yelled Jason.

But Skinner didn't wait. Lightning struck, and thunder roared again. The storm was getting worse. Skinner said something as he walked out the door, but Jason heard only thunder.

Jason watched as Skinner became a shadowy figure under the umbrella again. Then the lights of Skinner's car blinked on. They disappeared as he drove off in the downpour.

I should have stopped him, Jason thought. How could he just leave like that?

Jason wiped tears from his eyes and pounded the counter with his fists. The thunder rolled again.

A few moments later, another pair of lights pierced the darkness. The door flew open, letting in the wind and rain again. This time it was a policeman.

"How's it going?" asked the policeman. He stamped his feet on the mat as Skinner had done. "Boy, it's sure miserable out there tonight."

"Yeah," said Jason. He sat back down on his stool.

"Haven't had any visitors tonight, have you?"

"Visitors?" said Jason. He reached into the basin where he had thrown the wet rag and began wiping the counter with it again.

"We're looking for an escaped prisoner. We got a bulletin on him today. He's been in prison for twenty years. They think he's got some family around here."

The police officer took a cup and poured some stale coffee into it. He sipped the coffee and looked at Jason.

"Haven't seen anybody strange around here, have you?"

Jason finished wiping the counter and picked up the mop bucket.

"No, I don't get many customers in here after midnight. Nothing much happens on a rainy night like this."

Jason took the mop and wiped the puddle of water next to the magazine rack.

Word Study

aisle (I'll) a passage in a store, restaurant, or theater for people to walk through:
Please do not block the *aisle* with that large box.

diner (DIE ner) a small restaurant that looks like a railroad car:
We had a quick lunch at the *diner*.

festival (FES tuh vul) a time for celebrating marked by special events:
In the fall, our town has a *festival* to celebrate the harvest.

nightmare (NITE mare) a scary dream that usually awakens the sleeper:
She was so afraid of having a *nightmare* that she stayed awake all night.

saucer (SAW ser) a small plate on which a cup is placed at the table:
She rested the spoon in the *saucer* after she stirred her tea.

scribbled (SKRIB uld) wrote quickly or carelessly:
Dr. Douglas *scribbled* the prescription as he talked.

6. The Right Thing to Say

Ray played with the napkin in front of him. He took another sip of his coffee. She was late. But she was always late. At least it seemed to him that she was always late. He put the napkin in his saucer. He couldn't see it, but there was a small crack in his cup. Every time he took a sip from his cup, a tiny bit leaked. The napkin turned brown in the saucer.

Liz walked up to Ray's booth. She put her purse down on the seat opposite Ray and sat down.

"Hi," she said.

Ray took another sip of coffee.

"Do you want some coffee?" he said. "Do you want something to eat?"

"Coffee's fine," answered Liz. "Just coffee."

Ray looked around for the waitress. It was almost 11:00. The small diner was starting to fill up. He wished Liz had picked a less crowded place to meet. The waitress appeared and put a glass of water in front of Liz. "Can I help you?" the waitress asked Liz.

"Just coffee, thanks."

The waitress took the menus from Ray and hurried off. She hated people who ordered just coffee. They sat the longest and left the smallest tips.

"Why did you pick this place, Liz? You know how crowded this place gets. The club is almost empty this time of day. Why don't we go to the club?" he asked.

Liz put her hands around the glass of water. It felt good. It was July, and it was hot outside.

37

"Oh, I wanted to be someplace public, Ray. There are a couple of things I wanted to say." She looked at her glass. Water was running down the outside of it in streams. She took a napkin from the dispenser and put the glass on top.

"I wanted to tell you something," she said again. "And I wanted to be in a public place." She paused again.

The waitress came and wiped the table again. She placed the coffee cup and saucer in front of Liz. She scribbled on the check and put it next to Ray. She smiled.

"Call me if you change your mind about food," she said. She walked away.

"We've been dating now for six months," Liz said. "We've had some good times. I'm not saying that I haven't had a good time. The Neil Diamond concert. We really had a good time there. Then there was the art festival."

"Yeah, that was great. You know that painting I bought? I've gotten a lot of compliments on it. Everyone who comes over to my place thinks it's great. I'd like to buy another for the bedroom. I can't afford it right now, but next time—" He stopped talking because he could tell that she wasn't listening.

Liz turned the glass of water on the napkin.

Ray turned his coffee cup in the saucer. The napkin was completely soaked now.

"It's not like we haven't had a good time, but we really don't have that much in common." She leaned back against the booth. The cool vinyl felt good against her back. Her car air conditioner wasn't working very well.

"There have been some bad times, too," she went on.

"Remember the Italian restaurant? When you were trying to cut your sausage, and it flew into my lap?"

Ray laughed and leaned back, too.

"It wasn't funny then, Ray. It almost ruined my yellow dress. I didn't think the tomato sauce was going to come out. And you just laughed and laughed."

She started to smile. She didn't want to, but Ray could always make her laugh. He had one of those laughs that made other people laugh.

"Stop it," she said. "It wasn't *that* funny."

"Yes, it was," Ray said, still laughing. "You should have seen your face. That was our first date, remember? Everything went wrong that night. The line was so long at the Tower Theater that we couldn't get in to see the movie. Then we almost had an accident on the freeway. I remember it all. Come on, smile."

Liz was trying to hold back.

"I offered to pay to have the dress cleaned," Ray said.

"That wasn't the only bad date we had," Liz said. "There was that time we went to the beach. We took my car, and you insisted on driving. You missed the turn into the beach parking lot, and you tried to make a U-turn in the sand. The car was stuck for two hours before you finally agreed to call a tow truck. I got the worst sunburn of my life. And I was cleaning sand out of my car for weeks."

Ray smiled and dropped his shoulders.

"Yeah, I have to admit, that *was* a nightmare," he said. "My arms and back were sore for days from trying to push the car out of the sand." He was no longer smiling. "What's that got to do with anything?"

"Well, I've been thinking, Ray. Our relationship isn't going anywhere. We've been dating for six months. It doesn't take that long to find out about people. It doesn't take that long to find out if you have things in common. People who have things in common have something to build on. We have nothing to build on. There's nothing there."

Ray leaned forward.

"Come on and say what you want to say," Ray said. "I think I understand, but say what you mean."

"What I'm saying is good-bye. I don't think it's worth it. We've had six months. I care about you, but not enough. I don't care enough about you to continue. I want to get on with my life."

"Is there someone else?" he asked calmly.

"There has to be," she said very softly, looking out the window. She looked back at Ray. "No, there's no one else. But I feel there *has* to be someone better out there. I don't mean better than you, just better for *me*."

"Yes, Liz. I think I understand. I understand very well."

"Oh my," she said, taking a deep breath. "I didn't think it was going to be this easy."

"We're both mature people," Ray continued. "If that's the way you feel, that's the way you feel. We had some fun. That's it."

He looked at her with no expression. His face showed no sadness, happiness, or any other emotion.

"Yes, I guess that's it," she said finally.

There was a long silence between them. Liz didn't look up from her coffee. It was cold now. She took a small sip, anyway. Ray drained his cup and motioned for the waitress to bring more coffee.

"I guess I'd better get back to work." Liz grabbed her purse and slid out of the booth. "I'll call you sometime. We can get together. We can still be friends."

"Sure," Ray said.

Liz was sorry she had said that about being friends. She knew it wasn't true. As she made her way down the aisle toward the door, the waitress glared at her.

"Coffee drinkers," the waitress muttered. "What a pain."

A tall, well-dressed woman moved down the same aisle. She carried a cup and saucer with her. She placed them next to Ray's and sat down next to him. Ray reached over and squeezed her hand.

"How did she take it, Ray? What did she say?" she asked anxiously.

"Well, I explained to her that we didn't have much in common. I told her that we didn't have anything to build on. She said she understood."

"Oh, darling," the woman said. She squeezed Ray's hand back. "You're so good with words. I thought she was going to make a scene."

"Piece of cake, sweetheart. You just have to know the right thing to say."

Word Study

develop (de VEL up) to treat film with chemicals to bring out a picture:
Did the man in the drug store say that they could *develop* your film?

innocence (IN uh sunss) freedom from guilt or blame:
To prove his *innocence*, the man showed proof that he had been somewhere else at the time of the crime.

lab (lab) *short for* laboratory; a building or room where scientific work is done:
I don't know how to develop pictures, so I sent my film to the photo *lab*.

private detective (PRY vut de TEK tiv) a person whose business is finding information, usually to solve crimes:
The *private detective* helped the police identify the murderer.

scanned (skand) looked quickly or casually:
I *scanned* the front section of the newspaper for the story about the fire.

sentimental (sen tuh MEN tul) having a lot of emotion or feeling:
He wrote a *sentimental* poem for his sweetheart.

shuffle (SHUF ul) put in a random order; jumble:
It's your turn to *shuffle* the cards.

stacking (STAK ing) arranging in a pile:
Robert is *stacking* the empty boxes in the garage.

7. Pictures of Innocence

Phillip Adair pressed the doorbell several times. He stepped back and checked the small piece of paper in his hand. He wondered if the woman at the photo lab had given him the right address. A young woman answered the door and smiled broadly at the stranger.

"Yes?"

"I'm sorry to bother you, Ms. Adams." Phillip Adair tried to step forward. She blocked his way. "My name is Connors. The photo lab gave me your name and address. I'm afraid there's been a mistake."

"Mistake?" she said. She folded her arms in front of her.

"Yes. The pictures you picked up this afternoon from the photo lab are mine. Somehow the lab mixed up our pictures. I got your pictures, and you got mine."

"Oh, yes. *Those* pictures. Come in, Mr. Connors. Come in. I have them here somewhere." She stepped aside, and he entered the apartment.

"I know this might sound strange, but I really need those pictures. They have sentimental value. I'm sure you understand, don't you?" Phillip Adair looked at her, his hands in his pockets.

"Yes, yes. Sentimental value. Of course, Mr. Connors. I knew there had to be a mistake. I don't know a soul in any of those pictures. I was going to take them back when I had a chance. Please come in and sit down."

She closed the front door, but did not lock it.

"Now, let me see," she went on. "Where did I put those pictures?" She glanced around the living room. "I came in. I put my purse down over there." She pointed to an empty chair in the corner. "I put my keys over here on the counter, like I always do."

"Can I help you look for them?" Phillip offered. He had sat down on the couch, but got up suddenly. "I really am in quite a hurry."

She threw her hands up in the air.

"I just don't know where I put things. I'm going to get organized one of these days." She motioned for him to sit down again. "No, really, Mr. Connors. I don't need your help. I know I put them in a safe place. I'll think of it in just a second. They might be in the stack of papers on my desk."

She walked over to a desk in the corner of the room. It was covered with papers. She began looking through them, then stopped.

"Can I offer you a cup of coffee?" she asked.

"No, thank you," said Phillip. He got up from the couch. "The pictures, please, Ms. Adams."

"Call me Hillary." She started unstacking papers on her desk. She threw some on the desk chair. Others, she placed neatly on the floor. "Well," she said as she looked through the papers. "You must have gotten a surprise when you saw *my* pictures."

"Yes, I have them right here," Phillip Adair said. He reached into the breast pocket of his coat and brought out a package. He remembered looking at the pictures. They were mostly group shots of people eating and laughing in a restaurant.

"They're from a party I went to last week," Hillary said. She continued stacking and unstacking from the mountain of papers on her desk. "A friend of mine turned forty. Actually, he's my boss. You can't really be friends with your boss, can you? Well, we gave him a party. He's depressed about turning forty. He tells everyone he's thirty-nine."

"The pictures, Ms. Adams. I need those pictures."

"Yes, the pictures," said Hillary. She began all over again, stacking and unstacking the same papers. "They have to be in this stack. I just had them in my hand. Oh, here they are!" She handed the package of pictures to Phillip. "Please forgive the way this place looks, Mr. Connors. I've been working a lot of overtime lately. There are only twenty-four hours in a day, you know?"

Phillip snatched the package from Hillary's hand and started to shuffle the pictures.

"There seems to be a problem," he said. When he had looked at all the pictures twice, he looked up at Hillary.

"These aren't my pictures," Phillip said. He reached inside his coat again. This time he brought out a short-barreled pistol. He threw the pictures on the coffee table. Anger filled his face. He pointed the gun at Hillary.

"I *thought* I recognized you," Hillary said, backing away from him. She stopped when she hit the edge of the desk. "You're the guy who's wanted for murder. You killed that private detective."

"You're right, Hillary. My name isn't Connors. It's Adair." He stepped towards her. "Now, where are the pictures?"

"Why do you want those pictures so badly?" Hillary asked.

Adair shrugged his shoulders.

"The pictures are the reason I killed Connors," he said. "My wife thought I was having an affair. She hired Connors to follow me. One night, he trailed me to the house of a drug dealer friend of mine and spied on us

45

through a window. The next day, my wife was all tears and kisses because Connors told her I wasn't having an affair."

Phillip Adair paused and smiled. "I'm not boring you, am I?" he asked. Hillary shook her head "no," and Adair went on. "I went to see Connors. He said he'd seen me make a deal for some heroin. He acted scared at first, then he wanted money to keep quiet. I shot him."

Hillary swallowed hard.

Adair went on. "As Connors lay dying, he told me he'd gotten some pictures of me with the heroin, and that he'd already taken the film to be developed. But he wouldn't tell me where the film was. If the cops get ahold of those pictures, they can prove I had reason to kill Connors. I've been tracking those pictures down for a week."

He raised the gun. "Connors made a big mistake, Hillary. Don't make the same one."

Hillary folded her arms in front of her.

"This time, Mr. Adair, I think *you've* made the mistake." She looked toward the front door and called out, "Isn't that right, Lieutenant?"

Lieutenant Henry Trask, gun drawn, came through the front door, followed by several other officers. They gathered around Phillip Adair.

"Yes, Hillary," Trask said. "I think Mr. Adair has made a serious mistake."

Phillip Adair dropped his gun and slowly raised his hands above his head. "I don't get it," he said.

"My name isn't just Hillary Adams, Mr. Adair. It's Officer Adams. I'm the cop who found Connors where you left him to die. He was able to tell me where he'd sent that film."

"So, why'd you bother to make me confess? You already had the proof you needed," Adair said.

Hillary smiled.

"Not exactly," she said. "Poor Connors was a rotten photographer. The pictures all came out blank."

Word Study

commend (kuh MEND) praise:
 The principal wished to *commend* Mrs. Howard for her 10 years of loyal service.

concentrated (KON sen tray tud) thought hard; focused attention on:
 Richard *concentrated* on the chapter questions when he studied for the exam.

impressed (im PREST) affected strongly; influenced:
 Sylvia *impressed* everyone on the committee with her friendliness.

misjudged (mis JUDJD) had a wrong opinion of:
 We *misjudged* the distance between the two cities.

relief (ree LEEF) the removal of something painful, difficult, or unpleasant:
 Take two aspirins for *relief* of headache pain.

scholarship (SKOL er ship) a gift of money to a student to pay for schooling:
 Gene won a basketball *scholarship* to the University of Texas.

superior (su PEER ee er) having better quality; excellent:
 That stereo has *superior* sound for less money.

8. The Last Hope

Ron twisted the knob on his locker. He concentrated on the numbers and hoped his friend George would go away.

"What do you think, Ron?" George shifted his weight from one foot to the other. "Don't just stand there playing with your locker. Are you going to lend me the paper or not?"

Ron kept twisting the knob on the locker. Sometimes the lock worked well, and sometimes it didn't. He tried to remember the last number in his combination. "Quiet, George. I'm thinking. I'm thinking."

George put his books down and put his hands on his hips.

"What's there to think about?" he said. "You either lend me the paper, or I fail government. If I fail government, I won't graduate. If I don't graduate, my father will kill me."

"George," said Ron, finally getting his locker open. "Just because we have different teachers for government, that doesn't mean we can hand in copies of the same paper. What if *your* teacher and *my* teacher talk to each other? What if they find out that two students in two different classes wrote on exactly the same subject?"

"You've got Mr. Christian, right? Do you know how many students Mr. Christian has? He won't even *remember* your paper, let alone talk about it to my teacher over lunch."

"George, if we get caught, we'll be in a bunch of trouble."

49

"We're not going to get caught. Remember when I helped you with those math problems? Remember, you said you would have failed geometry? Remember, you said that you'd do anything for me? Remember that?" George was almost shouting. The bell rang for class.

"Don't raise your voice. I can hear you," Ron said. He took his British literature book from his locker and slammed the door shut. He wished that he had never made friends with George. He wished that he had never asked for George's help in geometry class last semester. He would rather have failed the class. It would have been so much simpler now.

"I remember your helping me. I remember promising to return the favor. I didn't think you were going to ask me to cheat."

"We're not going to get caught. Listen, you've got to help me. You're my last hope."

George didn't have his hands on his hips anymore. He looked at the floor as he talked to Ron. It made Ron feel terrible that his friend was asking him to cheat. It made him feel worse that they might get caught.

"I can help you write the paper if you want," offered Ron.

"Naw, I can't write. And, anyway, it's too late. The paper's due tomorrow. And Mr. Smith doesn't accept late papers, period. No excuses."

Ron reached into his notebook and pulled out the folder where he had his report. "Just be sure you get it back to me tomorrow morning so I can hand it in to Mr. Christian."

Ron watched as George slipped the report into his notebook.

"I don't feel good about this at all," Ron said.

"Thanks, pal," said George, and turned to run down the hall. They were both late for class.

A week later, Mr. Smith pulled the stack of reports out of his filing cabinet. He placed them neatly in a pile on his desk.

"As you leave the class, please pick up your research reports. I've graded them. I was very pleased with the way they turned out. Some of you did an outstanding job. I especially want to commend George Williams on his paper. Mr. Williams, I'd like to see you before you leave, please."

The bell rang, and the class filed by Mr. Smith's desk to pick up their reports. Everyone came up except George. He waited in his seat until the others were gone. Then he slowly walked toward Mr. Smith's desk.

"George, I want to congratulate you on a fine paper. You know, sometimes we misjudge people. I'm afraid I've misjudged you."

"What do you mean, Mr. Smith?" George's heart was racing wildly.

"I didn't think you were much of a student. From your test papers, I couldn't tell you were such a fine writer. In fact, I'm so impressed that I'm entering your paper in a contest we're having this year."

"Contest? I don't want to enter any contest, Mr. Smith," George said. "I just want my paper back."

"Don't be silly, George. The social studies department and the school are giving a prize for the best paper of the year. The prize is a five-hundred-dollar scholarship."

"I'm really not that smart."

"That's no way to think about yourself, George." Mr. Smith leaned forward. "In fact, I was talking to Mr. Christian about you this morning. He seems to think one of *his* students has the best paper. But I'm sure your paper is better than anything Ron Parker wrote."

"Ron wrote the other paper?" George felt a lump in his throat.

"Yes. Do you know Ron?"

"Mr. Smith, I really don't want to enter any contest. I really just want my paper back."

"All right, George," Mr. Smith shook his head. "If that's the way you feel about it, I won't enter your paper."

George smiled. Mr. Smith didn't move.

"I'm a little ashamed to admit this, George," Mr. Smith said. "But I was so sure that your paper was the best one—" He paused. "Well, I gave it to Ron's teacher to read yesterday. But don't worry. I'm sure he's finished reading it by now. He should walk in here any minute."

Word Study

antique (an TEEK) something made long ago, sometimes having great value because of its age:
That table is an *antique* that has been in my family for years.

breakable (BRAY kuh bul) easily broken:
If you plan to mail something *breakable* you'd better pack it well.

genie (JEE nee) in Arabian stories, someone with magical powers:
The *genie* could do anything except escape from his bottle when its cap was on tight.

nobleman (NOH bul mun) a person of noble rank:
The *nobleman* had to take care of anyone who lived on his land.

porcelain (POR suh lin) a fine, hard, white clay used to make pottery:
My mother gave me a complete set of *porcelain* dishes as a wedding gift.

[blend with the] scenery *slang for* fit in, look natural in a place:
I sure hope I can blend with the *scenery* at this party tonight. I hate being around strangers.

tarnished (TAR nisht) dull; stained:
You'd better polish the silver before our dinner guests come; it's all *tarnished*.

valuable (VAL yoo uh bul) of great value:
His friendship is so *valuable* to me that I would do almost anything for him.

9. The Lamp

Karen pushed hard on the door of the antique shop. She stepped in and heard a buzzer. She saw a man sitting at a desk at the back of the store. He smiled at Karen, got up from the desk, and walked towards her. He took long strides and spoke before he reached the front of the store.

"Yes, may I help you?"

"No, thanks," said Karen. "I'm looking for a gift for a friend."

"Perhaps if you tell me something about your friend, I can help you," the antique dealer said.

"All I can tell you is that he brags about having a lot of antiques," said Karen. "He isn't a close friend. In fact, he isn't a friend at all. He lives in the apartment next to me, and he won't leave me alone. First he wants to borrow my phone book. Then he needs help working the washing machine. Then— Well, now he's having a birthday party. If I don't go, he'll just have someone bang on my door all night. So I'm stuck."

The antique dealer mumbled, "I see." He looked at his watch. "Well," he said. "Call me if you need help." He walked quickly back to his desk, shaking his head.

Karen looked around. There were glass cases filled with porcelain and brass objects. They looked expensive. In the middle of the shop was a table piled high with everything from swords to washboards. Some of the things on the table were dusty or tarnished. Karen figured these objects would be cheaper. She went over to the table and began sorting through things.

"How much for this sword?" she said, swinging the sword above her head.

"Please be careful with that!" the dealer said, rising from his chair. "It's six thousand dollars. It was owned by a famous Spanish nobleman."

"Oh, my," Karen said, putting the sword down gently. To herself she said, "I could rent Zorro for that much."

"Have you got anything a little less royal?" she asked the dealer.

The dealer came out from behind the desk.

"You might try looking at the things on *this* table." He held his hand out towards a table at the back of the store. The objects on the table were even dirtier and more tarnished than the ones Karen had been looking at.

"Thank you," she said, and went to the table. There, among the vases and metal bowls, was a brass oil lamp. She thought it might be one of those lamps with a cigarette lighter built into it, but it wasn't. Still, it might look nice if it were polished. And its price tag said $19.95.

"How come this lamp is so cheap?" Karen asked, holding it up for the dealer to see.

The dealer had gone back to his desk. He looked up with a tired expression.

"I bought it from an old cowboy at a rodeo. I don't know how he happened to have it, but he was happy to sell it to me."

"I'll take it," Karen said.

* * *

When Karen got home, she put her purse and the oil lamp on the kitchen table.

I can't give Joe that lamp without cleaning it up first, she thought. Even if I don't like him, his birthday present should look nice.

She took out a jar of brass cleaner and a rag, and sat down at the table. She took the lid off the lamp. She spread brass cleaner on the lamp and waited for it to dry. Then she gently rubbed the lamp with a paper towel. She whistled as she worked, and began to rub harder.

Suddenly, Karen noticed a cloud of mist forming. She thought for a moment that she had left something boiling on the stove. She blinked twice, shook her head, and went back to rubbing the lamp. Then she heard a voice coming from the cloud of mist.

"Well, what do you want?" said the voice.

"Huh? Who said that?" Karen said, jumping up from her chair.

"I said, what do you want?" the voice said again. "I'm the genie of the lamp. You woke me up." The voice yawned.

"I don't understand," said Karen. She stared at the cloud. The mist was clearing. When it was gone, a man in a cowboy outfit stood in front of her.

"Wait a minute," he said, looking around. "Where am I?"

"You're in my apartment," Karen said. "Now, tell me what you're doing here before I call the police."

"Look, lady. The last thing I remember, I was working for one of the cowboys in a traveling rodeo. One day he told me he didn't want to have to ride anymore. So I turned him into an old man. For some reason, that made him mad. So he tricked me back into that lamp."

The cowboy folded his arms and looked hard at Karen. "I repeat: What can I do for you?"

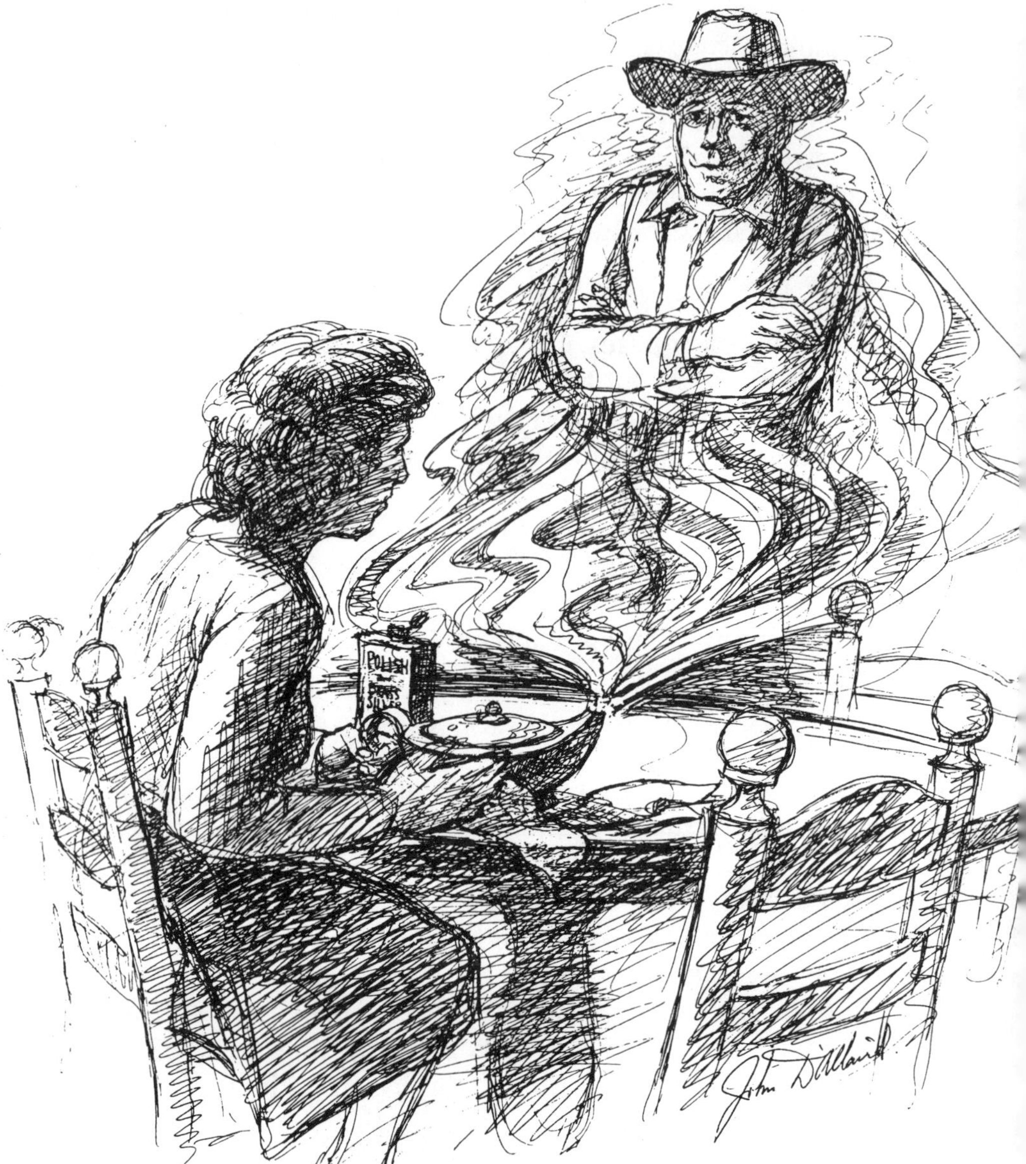
POLISH

A genie, Karen thought. I might just keep this present for myself. After all, what has Joe ever done for me?

"Are you really a genie?" Karen asked. "I mean, do you grant wishes?"

"More or less," the cowboy said, unfolding his arms. "Mostly, I do rope tricks."

He unhooked a coil of rope from his belt, and began twirling the end of it above his head. The rope swung across an open shelf over the sink, and knocked down a row of drinking glasses. Half the glasses fell to the floor and shattered.

"Hey!" Karen said. "Stop that. If you're a genie, prove it. Make my wish come true. I wish I had a million dollars."

The cowboy let the rope drop.

"Lady, if I had a million dollars, do you think I'd be living in this lamp? You ought to try it sometime. It's dark; it's smelly. And it's impossible to get anybody to fix the plumbing."

Karen was getting tired of this genie. And she was worried about her apartment. He was beginning to wander into the living room, twirling his rope. She had a lot more breakable things in her living room. She followed him.

"Why are you dressed like a cowboy, anyway?" she said. "Shouldn't you be wearing flowing pants and a turban?"

"I stopped wearing that stuff when I started with the rodeo," the cowboy said, sitting down on Karen's sofa. "I like to try to blend with the scenery, if you know what I mean."

He took off his hat and tossed it across the room. It hit a small table. A vase of flowers on the table shook and fell over, spilling water and flowers on the rug.

"Well, you can't stay here!" Karen said, running to pick up the vase before all the water spilled out. "The last thing I need is a clumsy genie who doesn't even grant wishes."

"Listen. I live in the lamp," he said. "I don't take up much space. I don't eat much. I do rope tricks. I help with the laundry. And, once in a while, I work a little magic." He stood up and looked around the room. "I'll show you. Look at the TV."

Karen looked at her color television set, sitting in the corner of the room. It was turned off.

"Watch!" the genie said. He waved his arms in a circle over his head.

Karen looked again at the TV. For a second, the screen lit up with bright colors. Reds and blues exploded across the screen. Then the screen, itself, exploded. Broken glass lay on the carpet in front of the TV set, and wires hung out the front of it. It was ruined.

"Oops," said the genie.

Karen tried to stay calm. She swallowed hard.

"You don't happen to have anything for a headache, do you?" she said.

"Why, sure," the genie said, pleased with himself. He started to walk back into the kitchen. Karen followed him.

"I'll have to go back in the bottle to get it, though," he said.

Karen watched as the genie faded, and a cloud of mist appeared above the kitchen table. The mist hovered over the old lamp. Then it went back into the lamp through the spout.

When all the mist was back inside the lamp, Karen clamped the lid down.

Just then, she heard a knock at her front door. She walked through the living room, past the smoking television, and put her face close to the door.

"Who is it?" she asked, not opening the door.

"It's me: Joe," said the voice on the other side.

"I'm getting dressed, Joe. What is it?" Karen said.

"I was just wondering if you had any lemons lying around, for the party," Joe's voice said. "Oh, and some potato chips. And do you have an ice bucket? Mine's an antique. I don't want to ruin it."

Karen sighed. "I'll look and see. I'll come over early to help you."

"Great! I need somebody to vacuum and hang the paper streamers."

Karen heard Joe walk away from the door. She turned and looked again at her broken TV set and the mess the genie had made of her apartment. Then she went into the kitchen to look for the things Joe needed. After she had found the lemons, the potato chips, and the ice bucket, she sat down to finish polishing the lamp with the genie in it. This time she made sure to leave the lid on.

When the lamp was nice and shiny, Karen tied a bright blue ribbon around its handle. Then she sat down to write a birthday note.

"Dear Joe," the card said. "I hope this gift shows you how much I value your friendship. Sincerely, Karen."

Word Study

cafe (caf AY) small, informal restaurant; coffee shop:
On Sunday afternoons, I like to sit in a *cafe* and read the newspaper.

genuine (JEN yoo in) real:
The jeweler guaranteed that the diamond was *genuine*.

merchandise (MER chun dize) goods bought and sold:
All *merchandise* in the store was sold at 50 percent off.

traitor (TRAY ter) a person who betrays his or her country:
The secret agent pretended to be a *traitor* so that he could find out the enemy's secrets.

valuable (VAL yoo uh bul) of great value:
Please be careful when you move that table because it is very *valuable*.

10. The List

Hansen entered the cafe. He walked to the booth in the corner where Krasner sat waiting for him. Krasner got up and held out his hand to Hansen. Hansen ignored the hand. They both sat down.

"It's good to see you, Mr. Hansen," Krasner said. "How long has it been? Four months? Six?"

Hansen pulled a pack of cigarettes out of his shirt pocket. He lit one and stared at its burning end for a moment. He was trying not to look nervous. He hadn't even heard Krasner. "What?" Hansen said.

"The last time, Mr. Hansen. Don't you remember?"

"Yeah, yeah, the last time. About six months ago, I guess," Hansen said flatly. "Did you bring the money?"

Krasner smiled. "Of course, Mr. Hansen. Did you bring the merchandise?"

"I have it right here in this envelope." Hansen tapped the right breast pocket of his coat. "Let's see the money."

Krasner smiled again. "I see we're not going to waste time being polite."

"I find it very hard to talk politely to a spy," Hansen said. "It's hard to be pleasant to someone who's trying to hurt your country." He immediately regretted what he had said. He knew what Krasner would say next.

"Mr. Hansen, *you* contacted *me*," Krasner said. "Also, may I remind you that *you* are the traitor? I'm just doing my job. I'm protecting the interests of my government. Nothing more."

Hansen stubbed out his cigarette. He grabbed the butter knife on the table in front of him and squeezed it.

Krasner hadn't said anything that he hadn't said to himself a hundred times already.

"Yeah, I know," Hansen said. "*I'm* the bad guy in this thing."

Hansen wished he hadn't lost so much money gambling. If only he could stay away from poker games, he thought.

"Where's the money?" he asked.

"Do I have to remind you that we are in a cafe?" Krasner said softly. "A hundred thousand dollars is a lot of money to carry around."

"Isn't your government willing to pay that much for a list of all the American agents working in your country?" Now Hansen was leaning forward and whispering. He knew the information he was selling this time was very valuable. "I'll tell you, it's worth a great deal to my government to keep it secret."

"Mr. Hansen," Krasner said impatiently. "Let's not argue. We've already agreed on the money. But I have to see the list to find out if it's genuine."

"Take my word for it," Hansen said.

Krasner took another sip of coffee.

"*Your* word, Mr. Hansen? The word of a traitor?" Krasner said. "Do you know that I could ruin you with a phone call? All it would take is one call to Mr. Rose, your boss. He would be surprised to find out that his good friend is a traitor. You do know that you can be shot as a traitor? They still do that in your country, don't they?"

Hansen's expression hadn't changed.

"Call him if you want, Krasner. Yeah, he'd be surprised, even shocked. He was my best man when I got married. We play golf on weekends. He got me my job. He also got me clearance to handle top secret documents. He might have me arrested. He might have me shot. But then, he might not do anything. After all, Rose wants to keep his job, too. If someone found out that the guy he brought into the agency was selling secrets to the enemy, it would look bad for Rose.

"What makes you think he wouldn't just get rid of *you*, Krasner?" Hansen went on. "Rose isn't afraid to have someone killed. He could arrange for you to have an accident. Accidents *do* happen, you know." Hansen smiled. He had thought of everything this time. He took the last cigarette out of his pack. He lit the cigarette and crushed the pack in his fist. "Now," he said. "Why don't we move our little party to someplace more private and get this over with?"

"I like you, Mr. Hansen," Krasner said. "You know what you want, and you don't care how you get it. It is a good way to do business."

Krasner slid out of the booth. He reached into his wallet and threw two dollars on the table.

"I have a red van parked at the northeast corner of the parking lot. Wait five minutes before you come out. I'll be waiting there for you, Mr. Hansen," Krasner said.

※ ※ ※

Hansen looked around the parking lot and tapped on the back door of the red van. Krasner opened the door. Hansen stepped in and closed the door behind him. Krasner pointed to a bench, and Hansen sat down. Krasner handed a large paper bag to Hansen. The money was in the bag.

"A paper bag? You're giving me all this money in a paper bag?" Hansen said.

"Count it, Mr. Hansen. I don't want you to feel cheated."

Hansen nervously fished through the bag.

"It's all here," Hansen said, folding over the top of the bag.

Krasner smiled and held out his hand, palm up.

"The envelope, please, Mr. Hansen."

Hansen took the envelope from his breast pocket and placed it on Krasner's open palm.

"Here," Hansen said. "That's a list of all the American agents operating in your country. That *is* the information you wanted?"

"Yes, it is," Krasner said, tearing open the envelope. He read down the list quickly.

"One thing," said Hansen. "How do you know the list is genuine? I could have put anybody on that list. How would you know the difference?"

"I know it is genuine," said Krasner. He pulled a gun from his coat. "I know it is genuine because it has my real name on it."

Krasner cocked the pistol. The back door of the van opened. A balding man in his late 40s stepped into the van. It was Hansen's boss, Mr. Rose. He sat down on the bench next to Hansen.

"I'm really disappointed in you, Robert. I thought you were smarter than this. I thought you had more respect for *me*."

Hansen just sat, staring at Rose.

"I've been watching you now for about a year," Rose went on. "Krasner is wearing a microphone. I heard everything you said."

Hansen hung his head.

"I can't tell you how much this hurts me," Rose said.

Krasner slipped into the driver's seat and started the van. He backed out of the parking space.

"Where are we going?" asked Hansen.

"Like you said, I want to keep my job," Rose explained. "If someone found out that my good friend, Robert Hansen, was a traitor, it would look bad for me."

Rose took a deep breath and sighed.

"What can I say, Robert? As you said, accidents do happen."

Word Study

checkered (CHEK erd) marked with squares of different colors or shades:
The woman wore a blue *checkered* skirt.

curse (kurss) a wish for evil or harm to happen to someone:
Eddie blamed his bad luck on a *curse* put on his family.

fortune (FOR chun) destiny; fate:
I learned to accept my *fortune* in life many years ago.

fraud (frawd) someone who is not really what they pretend to be:
That man claims to be a jewel expert. But I know he's a *fraud*, because he said my glass beads were diamonds.

Gypsy (JIP see) a member of a wandering tribe of people, believed to have come from India long ago:
Did you ask the *Gypsy* to tell your fortune?

insulted (in SUL tud) offended:
Tom *insulted* his girlfriend by picking her up two hours late.

superstitious (soo per STISH us) believing in forces beyond our understanding, like luck:
She was so *superstitious* that she wouldn't even leave the house on Friday the 13th.

uncontrollably (un kun TROH luh blee) not able to be controlled:
I laughed *uncontrollably* when the movie hero got hit in the face with a cream pie.

11. The Funny Man

Larry pushed aside the flap on the carnival tent. He and his brother, Warren, went inside. In the tent was a small table with chairs around it. Warren and Larry sat down at the table. It was covered by a checkered tablecloth. A small crystal ball glowed in the middle of the table.

"You know, I think this is a stupid idea," said Warren. "Five dollars thrown away."

"Shut up, will you, Warren?" Larry said. "Here she comes."

The old Gypsy woman opened a flap on the other side of the tent. She looked at Warren and frowned.

"Good evening, gentlemen," she said. "I am Madame Sosostris. I see you are curious about the future. You have come to see what lies ahead." She sat down at the table across from them.

"I'm sure you know what 'lies' are ahead," laughed Warren. "Get it? What 'lies' ahead?"

The Gypsy woman had been telling fortunes all day. She was tired. But she straightened in her chair and glared at Warren.

"Take it easy, Warren," whispered Larry, digging his elbow in Warren's side. "He didn't mean it, Madame Sosostris. He was just kidding."

"No, your brother wasn't kidding." The Gypsy stood up. "Perhaps it is better that you both leave."

"I paid my five dollars," said Larry. "That's what it says on the front of the tent out there. 'Fortunes told for five dollars.'"

The Gypsy sat down again.

"Very well," she said.

69

"I see you even have a crystal ball," said Warren.

"It's what everyone expects," she said. She shrugged her shoulders.

Warren picked up the ball and turned it over.

"This one's made in Japan," he said, laughing.

"Put that down!" shouted the Gypsy. "No one is allowed to touch the crystal except me."

"Put it down, Warren," Larry said.

"Your brother is acting foolishly," the Gypsy said, looking at Larry. "I will not allow myself to be insulted."

Larry turned to his brother.

"Warren, I want my fortune told," he said. "That's what we came in for. Do you have to make everything a joke?" He turned to the Gypsy. "I apologize for him, ma'am. He doesn't believe like I do. I'm sorry."

"Larry, I can't believe you're so superstitious," said Warren.

Madame Sosostris tried to ignore Warren. She took Larry's hand.

"I see you've been hunting lately," she said, looking at his palm.

"Yeah, how did you know? I love the outdoors," Larry said. He was impressed. "I'm not too crazy about hunting in bad weather, though."

Madame Sosostris traced another line on Larry's hand with one of her long fingernails.

"You will do well next season," she said. She touched a spot on Larry's palm. "Is there any sickness in your family?" she asked. She was frowning.

"No," Larry said, looking at his palm intently. "Do you see anything bad?"

"Nothing serious."

"Oh, you had me worried for a second," sighed Larry.

"This line here is—" she began.

"That line is dirt where he didn't wash his hands. That's what that line is," laughed Warren.

"Enough!" Madame Sosostris yelled. She walked over to the front of the tent and opened the flap.

"Please leave now," she said. "The man outside will refund your money. The session is at an end!"

"See what you've done, Warren?" Larry said, getting up. "You never take anything seriously. Even if she took the money and didn't tell us anything, *we* came looking for her. Not the other way around."

"Look, this woman is a fraud," Warren said. "She steals people's money."

"You will regret these insults," the Gypsy said icily.

"Don't tell me," chuckled Warren. "You're going to put a Gypsy curse on me, right?" He laughed out loud.

"You think that's funny?" Madame Sosostris looked hard at Warren. "You find everything and everyone amusing, don't you?"

"Yes," Warren said, still laughing. "Coming here was the funniest thing I've done in weeks."

"You will find out very soon that there is much sadness in the world. Yes, that's it," she said, stroking her chin. "Sadness. Much sadness."

Larry apologized again as he and Warren left the tent. They headed for the parking lot.

"You acted like a real jerk back there, Warren."

"Come on, Larry," Warren laughed. "You can't believe that stuff."

Larry looked down at his car keys as he opened the door of the car.

"I don't know, man," he said. "How did she know we were brothers? How did she know I went hunting last week?"

"She was guessing, Larry. Just guessing."

* * *

The office was too warm. Warren loosened his tie. Mr. Dotson, Warren's boss, looked at the column of figures on Warren's sales report. He avoided Warren's eyes.

"I'm sorry, Warren. But I've got to let you go."

"Why, Mr. Dotson? I'm your best salesman. No one sold more computers for our company than I did last year. This past month didn't go so well, but I'll do better. Just give me a chance."

Tears were welling up in Mr. Dotson's eyes.

"You were my best salesman, Warren." He wiped the tears from his eyes. "It's not even the sales. It's just that nobody can work with you without getting depressed. You used to make people laugh. Now," Mr. Dotson sobbed, "nobody can be around you without crying."

Mr. Dotson wiped more tears from his eyes.

"Please go now," he said. "I can't stand it anymore. Please leave!"

Mr. Dotson put his head down on his desk. He was weeping uncontrollably.

"I know what I have to do, Mr. Dotson," Warren said. "Things will be all right. I'll make you laugh again. I just have to go and apologize to someone. I'll be back."

"Please, just go away," said Mr. Dotson, not looking up.

* * *

Warren pushed open the flap on the tent, went in, and sat down at the table. He looked at the glowing crystal ball and tapped his fingers on the checkered tablecloth.

A flap at the other end of the tent opened, and a young woman walked up to the table and sat down.

"I see you're interested in the future," said the woman. "I am Madame Za Za."

She took Warren's hand.

"Wait!" he said, pulling back his hand. "You're not the one who put the curse on me. Where is she? Where's the one who was here last month? I have to talk to her!" Warren's voice cracked. The young woman began to sob softly.

"Please!" Warren went on. "I can't live like this anymore. No one wants to be with me. Everyone acts just like you're acting now. I went to the grocery store yesterday, and the checker started crying while she bagged my groceries. I've got to see the old Gypsy!"

"She's not here," the young woman said between sobs.

"Where is she? When will she be back? Please stop crying. You see why I have to see her? I'm even making *you* cry."

"Oh, it's not you," the young woman said. "It's just that Madame Sosostris died in her sleep last night."

73

Word Study

account (uh KOWNT) a record of money paid out, received, or owing:
Do you have a charge *account* at this store?

catalog (KAT uh log) a book or pamphlet with a list of names or objects:
Many people buy things through the mail using a *catalog*.

credit [a person's account] to place an amount of money in a customer's account:
Would you like a refund, or should I just *credit* your account?

desperately (DES per ut lee) hopelessly; dangerously:
I am *desperately* in need of a day off from work.

exchange (ex CHAINJ) give and receive in return:
I would like to *exchange* this dress for one in my size.

permanent (PER mun unt) lasting; continuing without change:
The catsup left a *permanent* stain on the rug.

receipt (ree SEET) a written record of money paid or goods delivered:
Did you save the *receipt* from your new washing machine?

security (suh CURE uh tee) safety; a person or thing that secures or guarantees:
The cat set off the *security* alarm when it jumped in through the open window.

supervisor (SOO per vie zur) a person who oversees and directs others:
My new *supervisor* is younger than I am.

12. The Receipt

Henry Fielding waited in line. He stood up tall to see if he was in the right one. He was. The customer service clerk turned the pages of a large book. She had a permanent frown on her face. It came from talking to angry customers all day long. She worked there five days a week, 50 weeks out of the year. Today the line in front of her seemed even longer and slower than usual. As it moved forward, she noticed Henry. He had a frown on his face, too. She took comfort in it the same way that most people took comfort in a smile.

"Next," she said, without emotion.

"Yes, my name is Henry Fielding. I received this package in the mail." Henry placed the heavy package on the counter. "I want to return it."

"May I see your receipt, please?" The clerk put the large book back in a stack under the counter.

"I'm sorry. You don't understand. I didn't come into the store to buy this. It came in the mail this morning."

The clerk looked at the clock. It was 11:45. At 12:00, someone would relieve her.

"Well, I'm sorry, too, because I can't give you your money back unless you have a receipt. I can't make an exchange without one, either."

"You don't have any of my money," he said calmly. "There's been a mistake. I didn't order this TV set." He patted the top of the package. "I don't need another TV

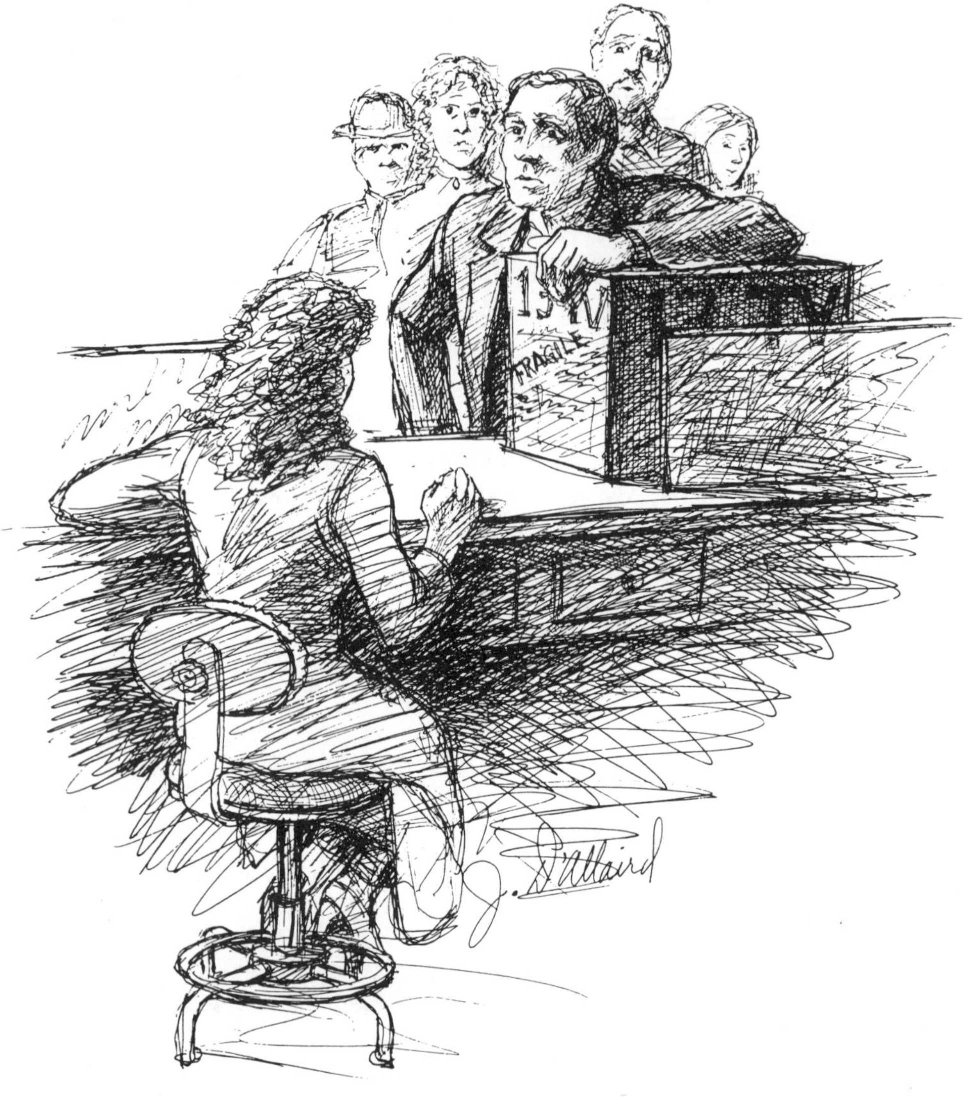
FRAGILE

set. I don't have any place to put another set. I don't want the set. Will you please take it back?"

"I'm sorry, sir, but you must bring in a receipt. It's the store policy. I have no control over that. I just work here." She looked up at the clock again. "If you've got a receipt, then we can do business. If you don't, then step out of line. There are other people waiting. Next!"

The line started to inch forward, but Henry wasn't moving.

"Just one moment. Just wait a minute!" Henry said. "The sign says Customer Service, and I want some service!" Henry was trying to remain calm. "I want to see the manager of this department, and I want to see him now!"

The clerk turned and picked up a telephone.

"Mr. Stevens, please come to the customer service desk. Mr. Stevens to customer service."

Henry heard the announcement boom over the store intercom.

"He'll be here in a second," she said. She pushed the package to the side and said, "Next."

A few minutes later, a tall, thin man came out of a back office. He was wearing a well-practiced smile.

"Yes, Mary," he said. "What's the problem? I'm busy right now."

"It's this man, here. He insists on returning something without a receipt."

"As I tried to explain," Henry broke in. "I received this TV set in the mail. I didn't order it. I'm bringing it back."

"I apologize for the store, sir. That must be a catalog item. If you will take that over to the catalog department, I'm sure they'll be glad to help you."

Henry shook the tall man's hand.

"Thank you, Mr. Stevens," he said. "I hate to bother you, but sometimes only the boss can help."

"You're welcome, sir," replied the thin man. He disappeared back into the office as Henry picked up the TV set.

Henry walked to the catalog desk. He had to stop once to grab the heavy package in a different place. His arms were tired. Fortunately, there was no line at the catalog desk.

"Excuse me," puffed Henry as he placed the package on the counter. "My name is Henry Fielding. I received this package in the mail, and I want to return it."

"May I see your receipt, please?" asked the clerk.

"I don't have a receipt," said Henry, out of breath. "Mr. Stevens over in customer service sent me here. He said you would help me."

"Well, I'll try to find a copy of the order, since you have no receipt," she said.

"No, no. You still don't understand. I didn't order it. You're not going to find a copy of the order. There *is* no order!"

"There's no need to get upset," said the smiling clerk. "Just as soon as we locate the order, we can give you a refund."

"But I didn't buy anything," said Henry desperately. "How are you going to give me a refund? I didn't pay for anything!"

"We can always credit your account, Mr. Fielding."

"I don't have an account at this store!" Henry shouted. "I just want to give something back that doesn't belong to me!"

The clerk held up a finger.

"Excuse me for a moment," she said. "I'll have to ask my supervisor how to handle this."

The clerk turned and disappeared behind a gray partition. She reappeared a few moments later. She was shaking her head.

"I'm sorry, Mr. Fielding. My supervisor says that we cannot accept a return without a receipt."

"OK, all right! You win! I'll keep the set. No problem!" shouted Henry.

Henry grabbed the package once more and started walking toward the nearest exit. There was nothing left to do. Henry pushed on the exit door and felt a tapping on his shoulder.

"Excuse me, sir."

Henry turned and saw the store security guard in a bright blue uniform.

"What's the matter, officer? I was just leaving."

"Yes, I can see you were leaving," said the security officer. "May I see the receipt for that package you're carrying? Nothing leaves the store without a receipt."